we aRe JEWISH FACES

by Debra B. Darvick

APPLES & HONEY PRESS

A Note from the Author

Visiting my children's day school many years ago, I was struck by the diversity of what "Jewish faces" looked like—children adopted from other continents, blue-eyed strawberry blonde sisters whose mom converted to Judaism, an African-American Jewish child, a sabra whose green eyes and olive complexion spoke of ancestors crossing many lands. The phrase "I love Jewish faces" came to me, inspiring me to write this book in celebration of Jewish diversity.

—Debra B. Darvick

Apples & Honey Press
Springfield, NJ 07081
www.applesandhoneypress.com

Copyright © 2018 by Debra B. Darvick
Adapted from I Love Jewish Faces, published in 2009 by URJ Press.

ISBN 978-1-68115-536-4

The author and publisher gratefully acknowledges the following sources of photographs:

Julie Lapin(boy Torah); Patty Bloom(bubbe, shofar, brass); Martin Darvick(zayde, challah, city, mt.); Brett Mountain(siblings); Hillel Day School(friendship, girl w/star); Naftali Hilger(Yemenites); Helen Yocheved Reinstein(tree); Behrman House(matzah); Abby Nelson (Purim); Erin Sternthal(lulav, writing); Lauren Goldman Marshall(menorah); Jamah Maman(nosh); Ali Reingold(hoop); Daniel Berkowitz(book, sad); Ashley Hooten(recess); Ann Koffsky(boy grad, pray); Andrea Arellano(girl grad); Hannah Markowitz/Gesher Jewish Day School (Yitzchak); Gary Donihoo (simcha); Rabbi Dan Horwitz(aunt kissing); Rabbi Michael Rovinsky(bris); Deborah L. G. Daniels(braces); Coleen Lou(4 girls); Cindy Haynes(stairs); Lauri Zessar(shuk).

I would like to express my deepest gratitude to the following school administrators for their unstinting help in my photo research. I couldn't have done this without you. Patty Bloom (Saul Mirowitz Jewish Community School); Gabriella Burman (Hillel Day School); Deborah L. G. Daniels (MetroWest Jewish Day School); Gail Lansky (Lander-Grinspoon Academy); Julie Lapin (Carmel Academy); Colleen Lou (The Epstein School); Ali Reingold (Hebrew Day School of Ann Arbor); Jennifer A. Scher (Gesher Jewish Day School); Erin Sternthal (Golda Och Academy).
—Debra B. Darvick

Library of Congress Cataloging-in-Publication Data

Names: Darvick, Debra B., author. | Darvick, Debra B. I Love Jewish Faces.
Title: We are Jewish faces / by Debra Darvick.
Description: Springfield, NJ : Apples & Honey Press
[2018] | "Adapted from I Love Jewish Faces, published in 2009 by URJ Press"--E-CIP title page verso.
Identifiers: LCCN 2017025346 | ISBN 9781681155364
Subjects: LCSH: Facial expression--Pictorial works. | Face--Social aspects--Pictorial works. | Jews--Pictorial works. | Portrait photography.
Classification: LCC BF592.F33 D373 2018 | DDC 296.7/2--dc23
LC record available at https://lccn.loc.gov/2017025346

Design by Alexandra N. Segal
Edited by Dena Neusner
Art directed by Ann Koffsky
Printed in China

9 8 7 6 5 4 3 2 1

We are **JEWISH** faces.

BUBBE faces,

ZAYDE faces,

BROTHER, SISTER,

FRIENDSHIP
faces,

faces
of all
RACES
and
PLACES,

we are **JEWISH** faces.

SHOFAR faces,

CHALLAH faces,

PESACH,

PURIM, SUKKAH
faces,

HANUKKAH MENORAH
faces,

we are **JEWISH** faces.

NOSHING faces,

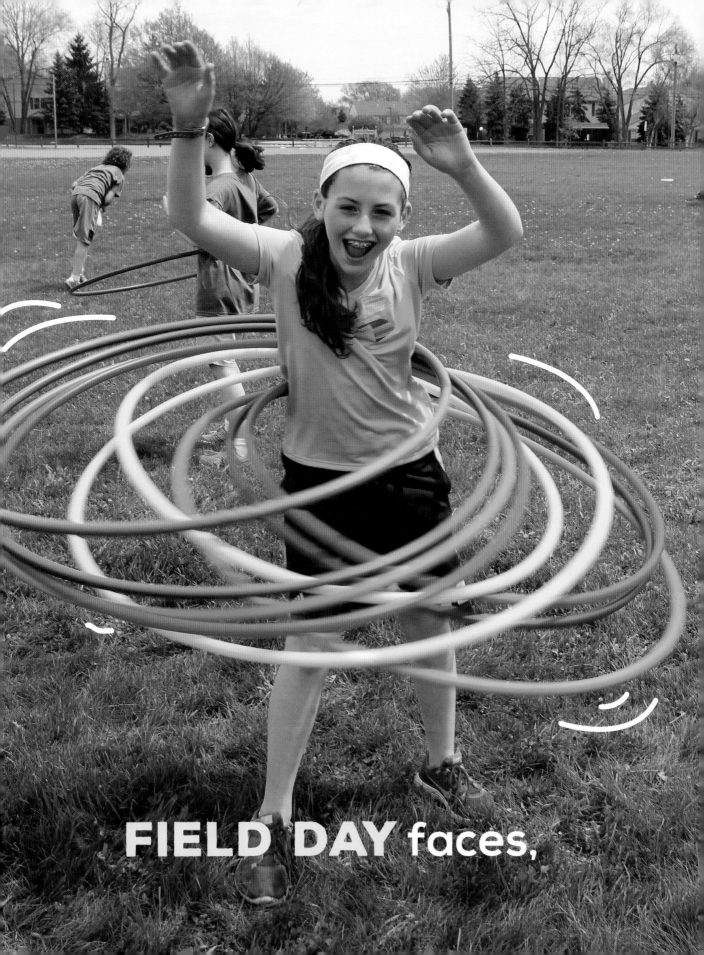

FIELD DAY faces,

WRITING,

READING,

RECESS faces,

smiling
GRADUATION
faces,

we are **JEWISH** faces.

SIMCHAH faces,

SORROW
faces,

MISSED and **KISSED**

and just-BRISSED faces.

This **BAR MITZVAH'S** wearing braces!

We are JEWISH faces.

In quiet PRAYING

or loud
BRASS PLAYING,

on
STAIRCASES,

in
MARKETPLACES,

from
CITY STREET

to
HIGH MOUNTAIN
SPACES.

We are JEWISH faces!